Rain Man

a novel by

LEONORE FLEISCHER

based on a screenplay by
Ronald Bass and Barry Morrow
and a story by Barry Morrow

Level 3

Retold by Kieran McGovern
Series Editors: Andy Hopkins and Jocelyn Potter

Pearson Education Limited
Edinburgh Gate, Harlow,
Essex CM20 2JE, England
and Associated Companies throughout the world.

ISBN 0 582 41785 6

RAIN MAN copyright © 1989 United Artists Pictures Inc.
A Novel by Leonore Fleischer based on a Screenplay by Ronald Bass and
Barry Morrow and a Story by Barry Morrow
First published by Penguin Books 1989
This adaptation first published by Penguin Books 1994
Published by Addison Wesley Longman Limited and Penguin Books Ltd. 1998
New edition first published 1999

9 10 8

Text copyright © Kieran McGovern 1998
Illustrations copyright © Bob Harvey 1994
All rights reserved

The moral right of the adapter and of the illustrator has been asserted

Typeset by RefineCatch Limited, Bungay, Suffolk
Set in 11/14pt Monotype Bembo
Printed in Spain by Mateu Cromo, S.A. Pinto (Madrid)

Published by Pearson Education Limited in association with
Penguin Books Ltd., both companies being subsidiaries of Pearson Plc

For a complete list of titles available in the Penguin Readers series please write to your local
Pearson Education office or contact: Penguin Readers Marketing Department,
Pearson Education, Edinburgh Gate, Harlow, Essex, CM20 2JE.

Contents

Introduction

'Raymond sees danger everywhere,' said Dr Bruner. 'Any change frightens him. That is why he always does things in the same way every day. He eats the same way, sleeps the same way, talks the same way. But he's a person, your brother. In some ways, a very intelligent person.'

When Charlie Babbitt's rich father dies, Charlie gets two surprises. One, he does not get his father's money. Two, his brother gets all the money. But Charlie did not know that he had a brother.

Raymond Babbitt is not like other people. He cannot live in the real world. He has lived in a home for many years. When Charlie meets him, he knows he has to fight Raymond's doctor to get the money.

But Raymond is someone special. When the brothers meet, it's the start of an adventure that will change them both.

Rain Man was the most successful film of 1988. Tom Cruise plays Charlie Babbitt and Dustin Hoffman plays Raymond. Before he made the film, Hoffman learnt as much as possible about people like Raymond. He talked to doctors and met many people with the same problem as Raymond. In the film, Hoffman shows Raymond's sad, strange world in a way that people all over the world could like and understand. He won the Oscar for Best Actor.

The idea came from a story by American writer Barry Morrow. He was a singer before he became interested in people with problems of the mind. Ronald Bass wrote the film with Morrow. He studied law, but now works full-time as a writer. Leonore Fleischer wrote the book of the film. She has written more than 50 books of films over the last 25 years.

Chapter 1   Bad News

It was Friday afternoon in the office of Babbitt Cars, Los Angeles. Charlie Babbitt was shouting on the phone.

'But I have waited five weeks for these cars. Where are they?'

On another phone, Charlie's secretary, Susanna, was talking to a customer. The customer wanted six Lamborghini cars and he wanted them that day. Then a call came from the bank.

Susanna put her hand over the phone. 'They want you to pay back the money you borrowed,' she said. 'They want it this afternoon.'

'Tell them I'll pay on Monday,' said Charlie. Then he spoke into his own phone. 'You can have the cars on Monday, sir . . . Yes, I'm sure . . . Thank you, sir!'

Charlie put the phone down and smiled for the first time in a week. Monday. And this was only Friday! He had the weekend to think of something to save his business.

He looked over at Susanna, his Italian secretary. She was his girl and she was so beautiful! Charlie loved every part of her little body, her big black eyes, her long brown hair.

'Are you ready for our weekend in Palm Springs?'

Susanna looked surprised. 'We're still going?'

'Of course,' said Charlie. 'Don't worry about this little problem. I'm going to make eighty thousand dollars from those cars.' He smiled his best smile. 'Not bad . . . for two or three phone calls.'

◆

They were driving through the desert when a call came through on Charlie's car phone.

'Mr Babbitt? Mr Charles Babbitt?' It was a girl's voice.

1

They were driving through the desert when a call came through on Charlie's car phone.

'Yes?'

'I'm calling for Mr John Mooney. He's your father's lawyer . . . here in Cincinnati. And . . . I'm sorry, but it's bad news. Your father has died, sir.'

'Oh, no!' Susanna said, her eyes on Charlie. But his face didn't change, and he didn't say a word.

'The funeral is on Sunday, Mr Babbitt. I've got his telephone number if you . . .'

But Charlie was not listening. He just continued to look at the road in front of them.

'Oh, Charlie,' Susanna said softly. 'Are you all right?'

He didn't answer, but a few seconds later he turned off the road and stopped the car. 'Sorry about the weekend,' he said finally.

'The *weekend*?' Susanna said. 'Charlie –'

Charlie did not look at her. 'Look,' he said quietly, 'I hated my father and he hated me.'

Susanna looked across at him. Charlie was only twenty-six, but she thought he was the most handsome man in the world. He was tall and strong, with thick dark hair and a wonderful smile.

'Poor Charlie! That's very sad.'

'My mother died when I was two. And then it was just . . . me and him.'

adj. รู้สึกหวั่นใจ xo, รู้สึกกินงงน

Susanna bit her lip and touched Charlie on the shoulder. 'What happened?'

adj. เงียบ ไม่พูดพา เสียง, พดน้อย

Charlie was silent. Then he said, 'Nothing I did was ever good enough for him.'

'I'm going with you to the funeral,' Susanna said suddenly.

Charlie smiled. 'That's nice,' he said, 'but you don't need to.'

'I want to go,' Susanna said.

Charlie looked across at Susanna. 'I forgot who I was talking to,' he said, with a small, sad smile.

3

Chapter 2   A Map of the Past

Charlie Babbitt walked away from his father's funeral without looking back. Getting into the car beside Susanna, he said, 'We're going to stay in Cincinnati another night, OK? There's something I have to do before we go.' Charlie started the car.

'Where are we going now?' Susanna asked.

'East Walnut Hills.'

Walnut Hills is the richest part of Cincinnati. All the houses are big and very expensive.

Charlie parked the car in front of one of the largest, most expensive houses in Walnut Hills – Sanford Babbitt's house. 'This is my father's place,' he said.

Susanna got out of the car. 'Is this where you lived when you were a boy?' she asked, her eyes wide, full of questions.

'Yeah, but I left when I was sixteen,' Charlie said. He picked up the suitcases and carried them towards the house.

'I had no idea . . . you came . . . from all this,' Susanna said. This was a Charlie Babbitt that she didn't know.

But Charlie wasn't listening. He put the suitcases down and walked towards a car that was in front of the garage.

It was a 1949 Buick Roadmaster. It was light blue and everything about it was perfect.

'I've always known this car,' Charlie said in a quiet voice, 'but I only drove it once.'

Near the garage was a flower garden with some wonderful roses.

'Someone must water those roses,' said Susanna, who loved flowers. 'They're all dying.'

'I hate those roses!' Charlie said suddenly.

Susanna looked at him in surprise, but Charlie was already opening the front door.

◆

It was a 1949 Buick Roadmaster. It was light blue and everything about it was perfect.

Later that afternoon, Charlie and Susanna were looking round Charlie's old bedroom.

'You know that car in front of the garage?' Charlie asked suddenly.

'It's beautiful.'

'My father loved that car. The car and the roses. The Buick was *his* car and I could never drive it. But one day I borrowed it to drive my friends round town.'

'What happened?'

'My father telephoned the police. He knew I had the car, but he telephoned the police and said, "Someone has stolen my car". The police stopped us and took us to the police station.' Charlie's face was angry now. 'My friends' parents came for them after an hour. My father left me there for two days.'

'Two days!' Susanna said. 'And you were only sixteen. Poor Charlie!'

But now Charlie was picking up an old coat from a box in the corner of the room.

'Is that yours, Charlie?' Susanna asked.

Charlie didn't answer. He was looking carefully at the little coat. 'It's like a map . . .' he said, in a strange voice. 'A map of my past.'

'What are you talking about?'

'What?' Charlie looked over at Susanna and then back at the coat. 'Oh, I was just thinking . . . Susanna, when you were a child, did you have . . . secret friends?'

'Yes, I think everyone does.'

'What was the name of my secret friend?' Charlie asked himself. He tried to remember. 'Rain Man. That's it. The Rain Man. When I was frightened I held this coat and listened to the Rain Man sing.' He smiled. 'That was a long time ago.'

Susanna laughed and touched Charlie's arm. 'What happened to your friend?'

'I don't know,' Charlie said. 'I just . . . grew up, I think.' He turned the coat around in his hands for a few seconds longer. Then he threw it back into the box.

'Let's go and eat.'

♦

Charlie Babbitt and his father's lawyer, John Mooney, met in the dining-room that evening.

Mr Mooney put on his glasses and took some papers from his case. 'Before I read the will,' he said, 'your father has asked me to read you a letter that he wrote to you. Is that all right?'

Charlie did not want to listen to his father's letter. But he did want his father's money. 'Of course,' he said.

Mooney opened an envelope and took out two pieces of expensive paper.

' "To my son, Charles Babbitt. Dear Charles," ' the lawyer began. ' "Today is my seventieth birthday. I am an old man, but I well remember the day that we brought you home from the hospital. You were the perfect child . . ." '

'He wrote it,' Charlie said, with a very small smile. 'I hear his voice.'

' "And I remember too," ' Mooney continued reading, ' "the day you left home. You were so angry, and you had all these big ideas . . ." '

The lawyer stopped reading. He looked up at Charlie, but there was no change in the young man's expression.

Mooney did not look up from the letter again. ' "You did not write, or telephone, or come back into my life in any way. For all these years I have not had a son. But I want for you now what I always wanted for you. I want you to have the best life possible." '

Now Mooney picked up the will. Without looking at Charlie, he began to read.

John Mooney stopped reading and put the letter back into its envelope. The old lawyer seemed sad. Charlie did not say anything. He just sat there waiting for Mooney to read the will.

Now Mooney picked up the will. Without looking at Charlie, he began to read.

'"To Charles Sanford Babbitt, I give my 1949 Buick. I also give him my roses."'

Charlie moved anxiously in his chair. He did not like what he was hearing.

'"I am leaving my home and all my money to someone who is very important to me. Because this person cannot use the money, a friend will look after the money for him."'

Mooney stopped reading and looked up.

'I don't understand,' Charlie said.

'Your father's money, around three million dollars, will go to someone who cannot use it,' Mooney explained. 'Another person will look after the money.'

So Charlie Babbitt was not getting his father's house, or his father's money.

'What's the name of the person who is going to get the money?' he asked.

John Mooney put the will back into his bag. 'The will says that I cannot tell you.'

Charlie was beginning to get angry. 'Who is this person who's going to look after the money? You?'

'No, it isn't me,' Mooney said. The old lawyer stood up and picked up his hat.

'Who is it then?'

'I'm sorry, Charles,' Mooney said. 'I'm your father's lawyer. I can't tell you.' He walked towards the door and then turned to face Charlie. 'I'm sorry, son. I can see that you're upset, but –'

'Upset?' Charlie jumped out of his chair. 'I get an old car and some roses. Wonderful! And this man without a name –'

'Charles –'

'This secret person gets three million dollars!'

'Charles –'

'Sanford Babbitt. You want to be his son for five *minutes*?' Charlie shouted. 'Did you *hear* that letter? Were you *listening*?' Charlie was so angry, he could not continue speaking.

'Yes, sir, I was,' John Mooney replied, looking at Charlie straight in the eye. 'Were you?'

Chapter 3   Father's Secret

Charlie wanted that three million dollars. It was his money! But first he had to know who was looking after it.

Next morning, he went to his father's bank and talked to a woman there. He smiled his beautiful smile and lied to her. Five minutes later he had the name and address that he needed in his pocket. Dr Walter Bruner of Wallbrook Home, Ohio.

With Susanna next to him, Charlie drove the Buick out of Cincinnati. It was a hot July day and they had the roof of the car open. On both sides of the road were the Ohio hills.

'This is beautiful,' Susanna said. 'Where are we going?'

'We're going to see a Dr Bruner,' Charlie answered. He did not say another word.

Twenty minutes later Charlie slowed the car down and turned to the left. The new road was very narrow. On both sides there were big trees. 'This is the place,' he said, 'Wallbrook Home.'

'But why have we come here, Charlie?' Susanna asked.

'It's something about my father's will,' Charlie said. 'It won't take long.'

On the way up to the house, they saw a strange man. There was paint all over his face and he was smiling like a child. They got out of the car and walked up to the front door. A nurse came out to meet them.

'I'd like to see Dr Bruner, please.'

The nurse took them into a comfortable waiting-room.

'Could you wait here, please?'

The nurse left the room. Charlie jumped up and went through a door into another room.

'Charlie,' Susanna called. 'Where are you going?'

She followed him into the other room where a group of people were watching television. Others sat at tables, playing with children's games. Two nurses in white coats sat at the back of the room. Nobody spoke.

'I don't like being here, Charlie,' Susanna said. 'It isn't right! Let's go back to the waiting-room.'

◆

Twenty minutes later Charlie slowed the car down and turned to the left. The new road was very narrow. On both sides there were big trees.

Dr Bruner was a big man. He was about fifty-six, with grey hair and a calm face.

'Could you please tell me the name of the person who will get my father's money?' Charlie asked politely.

'I'm sorry. I cannot tell you that.' Just like Mooney.

'Why is it a secret?' Charlie left his chair and went over to stand by the window. 'Is this person . . . an old girlfriend of Dad's?'

From the window, Charlie could see the old Buick. Susanna was sitting in the back, enjoying the afternoon sun. A small man, carrying a bag, moved towards the car. He walked in a strange way, moving from side to side.

'Mr Babbitt, I knew your father from the time you were two years old,' Dr Bruner said softly.

Charlie turned. 'The year my mother died,' he said quickly.

'Yes,' said Bruner. 'Now, the will names me as the person to look after the money. But this hospital and I get none of that money. I am doing this for your father.'

Charlie was beginning to feel very angry. To calm himself, he turned back to the window. The man with the bag was now standing next to the Buick. 'And you want me to just forget about the money?'

'I think you have been upset,' Bruner said softly, 'by a man who never knew how to show love.'

Charlie knew that this was true. He did not know what to say. Outside, the man was taking a small notebook out of his bag. He began writing in it.

'I understand how you feel,' Dr Bruner continued. 'But there's nothing I can do.'

'I'll fight for my money, Dr Bruner,' Charlie said.

Dr Bruner got up from his chair. 'I'm sure you are a fighter, Mr Babbitt,' he said. 'Your father was a fighter. But I am a fighter too.'

Dr Bruner walked with Charlie out through the front door. The day was getting hotter, but it was still beautiful weather.

The little man with the bag was still standing by the Buick. He was writing in his notebook. Again and again he looked from the car back to the notebook. He did not look at Susanna.

'Raymond,' said Dr Bruner, 'go back inside.'

The man with the notebook was not listening. He continued writing in the notebook. Charlie walked past him and went to open the door.

'Of course, this car is not white,' Raymond said. He did not look up from his notebook. 'This is a blue car now . . .'

Charlie looked at Raymond in surprise. He was a small man of about forty. He looked clean and tidy, with short hair and very ordinary clothes. What was a little strange was that there was no expression on his face. There was no light in his small black eyes, and no movement in his mouth. It was a face that was neither happy nor sad.

Smiling, Charlie turned to Susanna. 'You know,' he said slowly, 'this car *was* white. My dad painted it blue when I was very little.'

'And, and,' Raymond continued quickly to himself, '. . . it cost an *arm* and a *leg*.'

The smile left Charlie's face. 'That's what my father often said – "an arm and a leg". How does this man know that?' he asked.

Charlie looked at the man called Raymond. Raymond looked up for a second. Then he looked at his notebook again.

'You come with me, Raymond,' Dr Bruner said. 'These people have to go.'

But Charlie was moving closer to Raymond. 'Do you know this car?' he asked.

Raymond began writing in his notebook and muttering to himself.

A frightened expression came across Raymond's face. He looked at Dr Bruner for help. 'I . . . don't . . . know,' he muttered.

'Yes, you do know this car!' Charlie said angrily. '*Why* do you know?'

'That's enough, Mr Babbitt,' Dr Bruner said. 'You're upsetting him. You're –'

'Charlie, please,' Susanna said.

Now Raymond looked from Susanna to Dr Bruner. He began writing in his notebook and muttering to himself.

'Babbitt Charlie. Charlie . . . Babbitt. Charlie Babbitt. 1961 Beechcrest Avenue.'

Charlie was astonished. 'How do you know that address?' he asked.

Dr Bruner spoke quietly. 'Because he's your brother,' he said.

'But I don't *have* a brother,' the astonished Charlie said. 'I *never* had a brother.'

Chapter 4   Raymond

Charlie and Dr Bruner walked through the flower garden and talked together. Susanna sat with Raymond, who was still writing in his notebook.

'What can I tell you?' the doctor asked.

'Where to begin? 'What does he write in that notebook?'

'He writes down things that he thinks are dangerous. Things like bad weather reports.'

'Why does he do that?'

'I think he writes dangerous things down to try and hide them. Raymond sees danger everywhere. Any change frightens him. That is why he always does things in the same way every day.'

'What do you mean?'

'Raymond always eats the same way, sleeps the same way, talks the same way. Everything. But he's a person, your brother. In some ways, a very intelligent person.'

Dr Bruner looked at Charlie for a second or two, then he continued. 'Raymond cannot have relationships with other people, and he cannot see the relationship between things. He talks to you, but he also talks to the car and the television. Everything is the same to him. Doctors call this sort of person autistic.'★

★ An autistic person lives in a special world inside himself. In some ways, he thinks like a very young child, and like a child he needs other people to help him live in the real world. But some autistic people can also do very special things. One of the best painters of buildings in the world is autistic.

Charlie thought about this. It was difficult to understand.

'And the most important thing is that Raymond can't *feel*. He cannot be happy or sad in the way that we are happy or sad.'

Dr Bruner stopped speaking and looked at Charlie. Charlie was biting his lip and looking over at his brother.

'What Raymond did with you today . . . that was very good,' Dr Bruner said softly. 'Very good. For a stranger.'

Charlie shook his head and laughed. 'The world is strange,' he said. 'Three million dollars! What's he going to spend it on?'

♦

It was late afternoon. Charlie was walking with Raymond. Susanna waited in the car. She thought that Charlie was saying goodbye to his new brother.

Charlie walked quickly towards the Buick. Raymond walked next to him.

'This is Daddy's car,' Raymond said. 'It was white. But now this is a blue car.'

Charlie got into the Buick. 'Get in, Raymond,' he said.

Raymond got into the car.

'Charlie, wait a minute!' Susanna said. 'Where are we taking him?'

'For a holiday,' Charlie said. He started the car and they drove away. Raymond looked back over his shoulder at the house that they were leaving. There was no expression on his face, but it was very clear that he was anxious.

'Don't worry, Raymond,' Susanna told him, 'you're coming back.'

Charlie said nothing.

Chapter 5   TV and Pizza

They drove back to Cincinnati. Raymond sat in the back of the Buick and watched the road go by. He said nothing to Charlie or Susanna, but muttered strange things to himself.

They went to a hotel, and took two rooms. Charlie showed Raymond his room.

'This is your room, Ray,' he said.

That was a big mistake.

Raymond looked around the room. 'This is *not* my room,' he said. There was a frightened expression on his face. 'This is . . . is not my room.'

'Just for tonight,' Charlie said.

'Until we take you home,' Susanna said.

But Raymond was very upset now. He was shaking his head from side to side and muttering to himself. 'Of course, I'm going to be here a *long* time. A *very* long time . . . Of course, they moved my *bed*.'

'Sorry, Raymond,' Charlie said. 'You like the bed under the window.' He started pushing the bed into its new place.

But Raymond was still unhappy. He started muttering about books. The only book in the room was a telephone book for Cincinnati.

'Charlie, let's take him home,' Susanna said. She liked Raymond, and she did not like to see him upset.

'He's OK,' Charlie said. 'Do you like pizza, Ray?'

'Do you like pizza, Charlie Babbitt?' Raymond knew the word 'pizza' because 'pizza' was a Wallbrook word. This calmed him a little.

'I'll ask the hotel to send a pizza up to your room,' Charlie said. 'We like pizza, don't we, Ray? We're brothers.'

'Charlie, he still doesn't look happy,' Susanna said. 'I don't

Charlie cut the pizza into tiny squares for him, and put each square on a toothpick.

understand why you brought him here. I think he wants to go back to Wallbrook.'

'Ray's fine,' Charlie said, 'all he needs is some TV and some pizza. What's on TV, Ray?'

Raymond looked at his watch. '*The Lucky Money Wheel*,' he told the watch.

'Great. Sit down, and you can watch it.'

Charlie turned on the television. *The Lucky Money Wheel* came on.

'You've got your TV,' Charlie said. 'You've got a pizza coming. Aren't things good, Ray?'

Charlie looked at Raymond and Raymond looked at Charlie, but there was no expression on his face.

'Do you ever smile, Ray?' Charlie asked.

'Do you ever smile?' Raymond repeated. There was still no expression on his face.

◆

Raymond sat on his bed and watched television. Charlie came in with a pizza.

Ray looked at the pizza and shook his head. 'What's the problem, Ray?' Charlie asked.

Raymond wanted to eat the pizza the way that he ate it at Wallbrook. Charlie cut the pizza into tiny squares for him, and put each square on a toothpick.

Charlie and Susanna went off to their room. Raymond watched a film. A man in the film told his son to turn the television off. Raymond got up and turned *his* television off.

Raymond continued to look at the television, but now there was nothing to watch. He heard the sound of another television in Charlie and Susanna's room. Raymond got up and went into their room.

Charlie and Susanna were in bed. They did not see Raymond

come into the room. Raymond sat on the end of the bed and watched the television.

Susanna saw him first. 'Charlie,' she said, in a quiet voice. 'Raymond is sitting at the end of the bed.'

Charlie sat up and saw that Raymond was watching TV and eating pizza. 'Raymond, what are you doing in here?' he shouted. 'Get out!'

Raymond got up and went back to his room. Susanna looked at Charlie with an angry expression on her face. 'Go and talk to him!' she said.

'What for?' Charlie asked.

'Because he's frightened,' Susanna said. 'He's never been away from Wallbrook before. You've upset him!'

Charlie got angry. 'Raymond is not going back to Wallbrook,' he said. 'He has to learn how to live in the real world.'

Susanna was astonished. 'What do you mean he's not going back to Wallbrook?'

Charlie looked away from her and bit his lip. 'I took Raymond,' he said quietly, 'and I'm keeping him until I get my money.'

Susanna's eyes widened. 'What money?' she asked.

'Dad left Ray some money. A lot of money.'

Money! Now Susanna was beginning to understand. 'How much money . . . did . . . your . . . father . . . leave Raymond?' she asked angrily.

Charlie looked away again. 'He left him his house and all his money,' he said. 'Three million dollars.'

Susanna muttered some angry words in Italian and jumped out of bed. Then she picked up her suitcase from the floor and threw it open.

'What are you doing?' Charlie asked.

'I'm leaving you, Charlie.' She was coldly angry.

'I'm leaving you, Charlie.' Susanna was coldly angry. She pushed her things into the suitcase.

Now Charlie was astonished. 'Why?' he asked.

Susanna pushed her things into the suitcase and pulled on her coat. 'Because you've kidnapped your brother for money,' she shouted.

'I have not kidnapped him! I just want my money. What's wrong with that?'

'Everything!' Susanna shouted. She looked at Charlie for a second and shook her head. Then she picked up her suitcase and moved towards the door. When she got to the door, she turned and looked at Charlie again. 'I did love you, Charlie,' she said sadly. 'But you are not the man that I thought you were.'

Chapter 6   Toothpicks

The next morning Charlie took Raymond to have breakfast in a cheap restaurant near their hotel.

A pretty waitress came to their table. 'Good morning,' she said.

Raymond read the girl's name on the front of her dress. 'Sally Dibbs,' he said suddenly. '460192.'

Sally Dibbs was astonished. 'How do you know my telephone number?' she asked.

Charlie was also astonished. He looked at Sally and then at Raymond.   = surprise

'How do you know her number, Raymond?' he asked.

'The telephone book,' Raymond muttered. 'In the hotel. The telephone book.'

'You read the telephone book!' Charlie said. He turned to the waitress and laughed. 'He remembers things,' he said. Then he asked Raymond what he wanted for breakfast.

'This is Tuesday,' Raymond said. 'Breakfast is coffee and cakes.'

'That's fine,' Charlie said to the waitress. 'We'll have coffee and cakes.'

The waitress went to get the food. Suddenly, an anxious expression came across Raymond's face. 'Where are the toothpicks?' he asked.

'We don't need toothpicks for cakes,' Charlie said.

Raymond shook his head from side to side. 'Where are the toothpicks?' he repeated. 'Where are the toothpicks?'

Charlie closed his eyes and counted to ten. 'All right, Raymond,' he said. 'I'll get you some toothpicks. But I'm also going to make a phone call. I want you to wait for me here.'

◆

Charlie was on the phone. 'Dr Bruner, this is Charlie Babbitt.'

Dr Bruner was silent for a second. Then he asked calmly, 'Where are you, son?'

'That's not important,' Charlie said. 'What is important is who I'm with.'

'You have to bring Raymond back, Mr Babbitt,' the doctor said.

'Yes, I will,' Charlie said. 'When I get my one and a half million dollars, sir. All I want is my half of the money.'

'I can't do that, Mr Babbitt. You know I can't.'

Charlie turned to watch Raymond. He wasn't at their table! Then he saw him: Raymond was looking all round the restaurant. He still did not have his toothpicks.

'Bring him back, Mr Babbitt,' Dr Bruner repeated. 'Bring him back now.'

'I have not kidnapped him,' Charlie said. This was something which worried him. Was Susanna right? Was Charlie the Businessman now Charlie the Criminal?

'I know you haven't kidnapped him,' Dr Bruner said. 'Raymond is not a prisoner at Wallbrook. He's always free to leave us.'

Charlie breathed more easily.

'But we know how to look after Raymond here,' Dr Bruner continued. 'We know what he needs. You do not know anything about Raymond, Mr Babbitt.'

Raymond was still looking round the restaurant for tooth-picks. Charlie watched him anxiously.

'I'm Raymond's brother,' Charlie said into the phone, 'and my lawyer says I can get custody of him. If you want Raymond back, give me my money.'

'It's not your money, Mr Babbitt,' the doctor was saying.

Charlie was not listening. He was waving to the waitress.

Raymond stood up quickly and knocked the box of toothpicks off the table. The box fell to the floor and broke open.

'Toothpicks!' he shouted and he pointed at Raymond. 'He wants toothpicks!'

'I cannot give you what you want, Mr Babbitt,' Dr Bruner continued.

At last Sally gave Raymond a full box of toothpicks. Raymond took the box back to their table.

Charlie was getting angry. 'Dr Bruner, you've made a big mistake!' he said. He put the phone down and walked over to where Raymond was sitting. 'We're leaving, Raymond.'

Raymond stood up quickly and knocked the box of tooth-picks off the table. The box fell to the floor and broke open. The toothpicks went everywhere.

'Oh, Raymond!' Charlie shouted.

But Raymond was looking down at the toothpicks on the

floor. 'Eighty-two,' he muttered. 'Eighty-two, eighty-two eighty-two. Toothpicks.'

Charlie shook his head. 'Ray, there's a lot more than eighty-two toothpicks down there.'

Raymond's expression didn't change. 'Eighty-two, eighty-two, eighty-two. Of course that's two hundred and forty-six. Toothpicks.'

Charlie turned to Sally Dibbs. 'How many toothpicks in the box?' he asked.

The girl picked up the box and read the number off it. 'Two hundred and fifty.'

Charlie smiled at his brother. 'That was very close, Raymond,' he said. 'Come on, let's go. We're going to the airport. I have to go back to Los Angeles.'

As they walked to the door, Sally Dibbs called after them.

'He *was* right! There were two hundred and forty-six toothpicks on the floor. The other four are still in the box.'

♦

At the airport Charlie telephoned his office. The news was not good. Both the bank and the customer for the Lamborghini cars were still very unhappy. Charlie needed to get back to Los Angeles fast.

Charlie picked up his bag. 'OK, Raymond,' he said. 'We've got to move quickly. Our plane leaves in six minutes. Look, there it is out there.'

Charlie pointed out through the window at the plane. Raymond suddenly looked very anxious.

'Crash,' he muttered. 'That plane . . . crashed in August. August 16, 1987. One hundred and fifty-six people were . . . They were all . . .'

'That was a different plane, Ray,' Charlie said. 'This is a beautiful plane. This one is safe.'

25

'Crash,' he muttered. 'That plane . . . crashed in August. August 16, 1987. One hundred and fifty-six people were . . . They were all . . .'

'Crash,' Raymond muttered. 'Crash and burn.'

Charlie did not know what to do. They had only four minutes to catch the plane. 'We have to fly home, Ray,' he said. 'It's important. What did you think we were doing here? This is an airport. This is where they keep the planes! Come on!'

Charlie put his hand on Raymond's arm. Raymond put his hand to his mouth and bit it. Then he screamed and began to shake all over.

For a second, Charlie just looked at his brother with an astonished expression. Then he saw that he had to calm Raymond down. 'It's OK, Raymond,' he said quickly. 'It's OK. We'll drive to Los Angeles. It will take three days, but we'll drive. No planes.'

Raymond stopped screaming. His body stopped shaking and slowly the anxious expression left his face.

'I'm sorry, Raymond,' Charlie said softly. 'I'm sorry I upset you.'

Charlie turned and began walking out of the airport. A second later Raymond followed him.

Chapter 7   Rain Man

Charlie drove all through the night. He felt tired and anxious. He needed to get back to Los Angeles fast to try and save his business. He was losing time that he did not have.

The next evening they stopped at a hotel. Their room had a small bathroom. Charlie went in to have a bath. Raymond was cleaning his teeth, and his mouth was full of toothpaste.

'Don't use so much toothpaste, Ray!' Charlie said.

But Raymond continued cleaning his teeth. Toothpaste came out of his mouth and dropped on to his shirt.

'Will you stop that, Ray!' Charlie said.

Raymond did not stop. 'You like it, Charlie Babbitt,' he muttered.

Charlie shook his head. 'No, I do *not* like it!' he shouted.

'You say, "Funny Rain Man . . . funny teeth."'

Suddenly Charlie stopped shouting. *Funny Rain Man.* Rain Man! That was the name of his secret friend when he was a child. 'What did you say?' he asked.

'You can't say Raymond,' his brother said. 'You're a baby. You say, "Rain Man". "Funny Rain Man".'

Charlie sat down on the side of the bath. He didn't know what to think. He was finding it difficult to breathe. 'You . . . you're the Rain Man?' Charlie said finally.

Raymond put his hand in his pocket and pulled out an

27

envelope. He opened the envelope and carefully took out a small photograph.

Charlie took the photograph and looked at it. A young man of about eighteen was looking at the camera, but not smiling. He was holding a baby in his arms. The baby was Charlie Babbitt, and the young man was Raymond Babbitt.

'Daddy took the picture,' Raymond said.

Charlie looked at the photograph for a long time. He was astonished. He and Raymond. Charlie and Raymond. Charlie and the Rain Man.

'And you . . . lived with us then? When . . . did you leave us?'

'It was Thursday,' Raymond said.

'Which Thursday, Ray?'

'It was snowing outside. Maria stayed with you when Daddy took me to my home. January 21st, 1965. On a Thursday.'

'That's when our mother died,' Charlie breathed softly. 'Just after New Year.'

'And you had your coat. And you waved to me from the window. Goodbye, Rain Man. Goodbye, Rain Man. On a Thursday.'

Suddenly Charlie remembered deep into his past. He remembered the snow. And waving to Rain Man. And later crying. Crying for Rain Man. He wanted Rain Man, but Raymond didn't come. He never came again.

'I sat with that coat,' Charlie said. Now he remembered his brother's eighteen-year-old face. 'And you sang to me.'

For a minute Raymond just looked at his brother. Then, very softly, he began to sing a song by The Beatles.

When Raymond finished singing, Charlie moved closer to him. Then he said, 'I remember I liked it. When you sang to me.'

But Raymond was cleaning his teeth again. Charlie picked up the photograph and muttered something about how nice it was. Then he put it down on the side of the bath and turned on the water.

Charlie put the photograph on the side of the bath and turned on the water. Suddenly Raymond began to scream.

Suddenly Raymond began to scream 'No, no, no, no!' Charlie looked up and saw a terrible expression on his brother's face. Raymond was looking down at the water. 'It's BURNING him!' he screamed.

Quickly, Charlie turned off the water. He remembered it all now. His brother giving a two-year-old boy a bath that was too hot. Sanford Babbitt screaming, *'He's burning Charlie! He's going to kill him!'*

That was why his father sent Raymond to Wallbrook. That was the end of the relationship between Charlie and Rain Man. And poor Raymond remembered it all.

'It's OK, Ray,' Charlie said softly to his brother. 'It's OK, man. I didn't burn. I'm fine.'

◆

It was late. Raymond was sleeping on one of the two beds in the hotel room. Charlie lay on the other bed, and smoked a cigarette. He felt very tired and very sad. He needed someone to love. Someone who loved him. He needed Susanna.

Charlie pulled the telephone towards him.

'Hello?'

'Hello, it's me, Charlie,' he said softly.

There was no answer.

'I . . . I just want to hear . . . that our relationship is not . . .' Charlie waited for Susanna to say something. When she still did not speak, he said, 'I'm frightened that it's finished between us.'

Finally, Susanna spoke. 'Don't ask me today, Charlie. You won't like my answer. Give me some time.'

'I'm . . . going to get custody of Ray. I've talked to my lawyer and he says that it is possible. Firstly, I have to take Ray to see a special doctor in Los Angeles.'

'Charlie, they won't give you custody of Ray,' Susanna said. 'Dr Bruner has looked after him for more than twenty years. You've known him for four days.'

She didn't understand. Nobody understood his relationship with Raymond. 'Can I phone you when I get back to Los Angeles?'

Susanna didn't say yes, but she didn't say no either.

Chapter 8   Las Vegas

The next morning Charlie heard more bad news from the office. They were taking the Lamborghinis away. And Charlie had very little money left. He was paying for everything with his American Express card.

Charlie and Ray sat together in the hotel restaurant. At the next table there was a group of twenty businessmen. They were finishing their meal and asked the waitress for the bill.

Raymond looked over at the table. It was full of plates and cups and different bits of food.

'Of course that bill is ninety-three dollars, forty,' Raymond said.

Charlie laughed. 'How can you know that, Ray?'

'Ninety-three dollars, forty,' Raymond repeated.

The waitress returned with the bill. Charlie read over her shoulder. The bill was for ninety-three dollars, forty.

'How do you do it, Ray?' Charlie asked. 'You can remember every number in a phone book. You can count two hundred toothpicks in under a second. You're like a computer.'

'Today is Thursday,' Raymond said. 'Thursday is coffee and cakes. Same as Tuesday.'

Charlie looked at his brother. Suddenly he had an idea. A really great idea to end all his money problems.

'Raymond,' he asked his brother. 'Have you ever played cards?'

♦

The next day they arrived in Las Vegas. Charlie bought new suits for Raymond and himself. He also bought Raymond a television the size of a small clock. Then he showed his brother how to play cards.

'Do you understand how to play now, Raymond?'

'I count cards,' said Raymond.

'Yes, but you must *never* say that.'

They went into the Golden Casino at four o'clock in the afternoon. They sat down at one of the card tables. Five hours later they got up from the card table. Charlie was very, very tired, but very happy.

He smiled at his brother. 'Raymond, you have won us ninety thousand dollars.'

Raymond did not look up from the television he now carried

They went into the Golden casino at four o' clock in the afternoon.
They sat down at one of the card tables.

everywhere in his hand. 'Eighty-nine thousand, seven hundred and fifty-six dollars,' he said.

And that was only in one visit! 'You're going to make us rich, Ray,' Charlie said.

Raymond looked from his television to his watch. 'Eight minutes to bed time,' he said. 'Eight minutes.'

Charlie smiled. Raymond was still Raymond. 'Ray, we're going to stay in the best room in the hotel here,' he said. 'Tomorrow we're going to come down and enjoy ourselves. Perhaps we'll find you a girl.'

Raymond was watching his television again. 'A girl,' he repeated.

'Yes, why not?'

But first Charlie needed a hot bath and a good night's sleep. And he needed to talk to Susanna again.

◆

There was a knock on the door. Charlie opened it. 'Susanna!' Charlie put his arms round the girl that he loved and kissed her. 'Ray, Susanna's here!'

'How did you know we were here?' Charlie asked her.

Susanna spoke softly. 'They told me at the office,' she said. 'I'm sorry they took the cars away.'

'Oh, don't worry about that,' Charlie said happily. 'We have some news to tell you. Ray, tell Susanna what we've done.'

'We played cards,' Raymond said. 'I counted cards and we won money.'

'What?' Susanna asked.

'It's a long story,' Charlie said, pulling Susanna towards the bedroom. 'We'll talk about it later.'

◆

Raymond knocked on the bedroom door.

'Come in,' Charlie called.

33

Raymond opened the door and stood there with his little television in his hand.

'Six minutes until I find a girl. To dance with,' Raymond said. 'You said ten o'clock.'

'A girl?' Susanna asked.

Charlie was getting out of bed. 'I taught him to dance. Now, we're going to try to find him a girl to dance with.'

'Five minutes,' Raymond said.

◆

They walked round the Golden Casino for an hour. It was very difficult to find a girl for Raymond to dance with. To other people Raymond seemed strange.

Charlie pointed to one of the tables. 'This is where we played cards,' he said. Suddenly, he felt a hand on his shoulder. He turned around to see two big men in suits.

'Mr Babbitt?'

'Yes?'

'The boss wants to see you, please,' one of the men said. He did not smile and Charlie guessed that there was a problem.

Charlie turned to Susanna. 'Can you take Raymond back to our hotel room?'

'Of course,' Susanna said.

Susanna and Raymond took the lift back to their room. Raymond was watching a film with Fred Astaire and Ginger Rogers on his little TV.

In the lift, Susanna looked at Raymond and felt sad for him. 'Raymond, have you ever danced with a girl before?' she asked.

'I've danced with Charlie Babbitt,' Raymond said. 'One time. With Charlie Babbitt.' He did not look up from his TV.

The music from the dancing below came into the lift. 'I like this music,' Susanna said softly. 'Do you want to dance with me, Raymond.'

Susanna stopped the lift between two floors. She moved closer to Raymond and took his hand in hers. They started to dance inside the lift. Raymond watched his television over Susanna's shoulder.

The song came to an end. Susanna started the lift again. 'The other girls have missed a beautiful dance,' she said.

Later Charlie came up to the room. He looked very tired. 'We have to leave here tomorrow,' he said. 'They won't let us play cards here again.'

'Why not?' Susanna asked.

'Because we won,' said Charlie, 'and they don't like people winning. I guess Raymond was too good for them.'

Chapter 9   A Very Good Driver

They left Las Vegas the next morning, and drove back to Los Angeles. Susanna sat next to Charlie in the front of the Buick. Raymond sat in the back of the car and watched another film on his TV. Sometimes he looked out at the desert they were driving through.

Once Raymond drove the car for a few minutes. The road was empty so there was no danger.

'I'm a . . . very good . . . driver,' Raymond said.

Susanna got out at her flat in Santa Monica. Charlie and Raymond drove on to Charlie's house in Los Angeles.

There was a letter waiting for Charlie. It was from Dr Bruner. 'I'm staying here in Los Angeles, at the Hotel California,' the letter said. 'Please come and see me. I think we need to talk.'

That night Charlie went to see Dr Bruner at his hotel.

'Mr Babbitt, I want to stop playing games,' Dr Bruner said. 'My lawyer is talking to your lawyer. He is explaining to him . . . the facts. Raymond will see a special doctor on Friday. This doctor will decide who gets custody of Raymond. And you are going to lose.'

'I think that is for the doctor to decide,' Charlie said. 'But I have helped Raymond more in one week than you have in twenty years.'

'You *think* you have helped Raymond!' Dr Bruner said. 'But Raymond is still autistic. He will always be autistic! Neither you nor I can change that fact.'

Charlie turned to go. 'I'll see you on Friday, Dr Bruner.'

'Don't you understand, Charlie?' Dr Bruner called. 'Even if they give you custody of Raymond, you will not get your father's money. I don't have to pay you anything.'

'Goodbye, Dr Bruner,' Charlie said, walking away.

Dr Bruner called after him. 'I'll give you two hundred and fifty thousand dollars to have Raymond back now.'

Charlie stopped walking and turned round to face the doctor. He shook his head. 'I don't want your money, Dr Bruner,' he said, 'I want my brother.'

♦

Friday came. Dr Marston sat at his desk. Next to him was Dr Bruner. In front of him were Charlie and Raymond. The two brothers were both wearing suits.

'There's no easy way to say this, Mr Babbitt,' Dr Marston began.

He did not need to continue. Charlie understood. 'You're sending Raymond back to Wallbrook,' he said.

'They can look after him there,' Dr Marston said. 'They understand Raymond's problems.'

'But Raymond has changed,' Charlie said angrily. 'He has only been seven days with me and already he is getting better. And you don't like that.'

Dr Marston and Dr Bruner sat silently for a minute. Then Dr Bruner turned to Raymond.

'How was your holiday, Raymond? Tell me what you did.'

Raymond held his little TV to his heart. 'I played cards,' he said. 'With Charlie Babbitt. And I drove Daddy's car.'

Dr Bruner laughed. 'You drove a car, Raymond?'

'It was on a quiet road,' Charlie said.

'And I danced with Susanna,' Raymond said.

Even Charlie was surprised at this.

Dr Bruner took a pen from his pocket and wrote something down in a notebook. Then he turned to Raymond. 'Do you want to stay with Charlie, Raymond?' he asked.

'I want to stay with Charlie Babbitt,' Raymond said.

'You see,' Charlie said. 'Raymond wants to stay with me.'

But Dr Bruner did not look at Charlie. He looked at Raymond. 'Do you want to go back to Wallbrook, Raymond?'

'I want to go back to Wallbrook.'

Dr Bruner wrote again in his notebook. Dr Marston also wrote something down.

'But what do you want to do, Raymond?' Dr Bruner asked again. 'Do you want to stay with Charlie? Or do you want to go back to Wallbrook?'

Raymond was now breathing very deeply. He shook his head from side to side, and moved uncomfortably in his chair. 'Wallbrook . . . Charlie Babbitt . . . Wallbrook . . . Charlie Babbitt,' he muttered.

Charlie jumped out of his chair. 'Stop asking him all these questions,' he shouted. 'You're upsetting him.'

Now Dr Bruner looked at Charlie. 'I'm showing you that Raymond is still autistic, Charlie,' he said calmly.

Charlie sat down and put his head in his hands. He saw that they would never give him custody of Raymond. Perhaps they were right. Perhaps they did know how to look after Raymond at Wallbrook.

Dr Marston turned to Dr Bruner for an answer. 'Of course you can visit Raymond,' Dr Bruner answered

But Charlie gave Raymond something they could not give him at Wallbrook. Charlie gave Raymond love. And Raymond, in his way, gave Charlie love.

All Charlie wanted was the best for Raymond. Charlie wasn't the loser. Raymond was the winner.

'Ray, they want you to go back to Wallbrook,' Charlie said slowly to his brother. He looked up at the two doctors. 'Can I visit him?'

Dr Marston turned to Dr Bruner for an answer. 'Of course,' Dr Bruner answered. 'We would like you to.'

Raymond took out his photograph. It was a lovely picture of the eighteen-year-old Raymond and the two-year-old Charlie. Rain Man and Charlie. Brothers. Raymond handed the photograph to Charlie.

Charlie began to cry softly.

'Are you all right, son?' Dr Bruner asked.

Charlie looked up and smiled. Then he turned to his brother. 'I'll come to see you, Ray,' he said. 'And you can drive Dad's car when I visit.'

'I'm a very good driver,' Raymond said.

ACTIVITIES

Chapters 1–3

Before you read

1 Look at the picture on the front cover of the book. Describe the two men. What does this picture suggest about their relationship, do you think?

2 Find these words in your dictionary.

anxiously astonished expression funeral
lawyer mutter notebook upset will

   a Choose the correct answer. A lawyer reads a *will* after
      (i) a birth   (ii) a wedding   (iii) a funeral

   b Make five sentences. In each sentence use *one* word from each box.

mutter	anxiously
upset	notebook
astonished	expression
will	will
lawyer	funeral

After you read

3 Choose the correct answer.

   a Susanna
      (i) has always known about Charlie's rich father.
      (ii) feels sorry for Charlie.
      (iii) talks to Raymond while Charlie is with Dr Bruner.

   b Charlie feels angry about the will because
      (i) he hates roses.
      (ii) his father has left him nothing.
      (iii) he doesn't know who has got the money.

   c Raymond
      (i) is about 14 years older than his brother.
      (ii) has small, blue eyes.
      (iii) has a sad face.

4 How does Charlie feel, and why, when . . .

   a the bank asks him for money?

   b he hears his father has died?

   c he finds a coat in his father's house?

   d he remembers his father's car?

   e Raymond talks to him?

   f Dr Bruner tells him about his brother?

Chapters 4–6

Before you read

5 Why has Sanford Babbitt left all his money to Raymond, do you think? Do you think he was right? Why or why not?

6 Find these words in your dictionary.

   breathe   custody   relationship   toothpick

   Put the right word in the right space.

   a wooden . . . . .

   b police . . . . .

   c . . . . . quietly

   d friendly . . . . .

After you read

7 In how many ways is Raymond different from other people? What examples of these differences can you find?

8 Why does Susanna leave Charlie? Do you think she is right or not? Why?

9 Work in pairs with another student. Act out this conversation between Susanna and Charlie.

   Student A: You are Susanna. Tell Charlie why you think that Raymond must go back to Wallbrook. When he tells you about the money, tell him why you're leaving.

   Student B: You are Charlie. Tell Susanna why you don't want your brother to go back to Wallbrook. Tell her about the money. Ask her not to leave you.

Chapters 7–9

Before you read

10 What does Charlie think of his brother at the moment? How do you think their relationship will change?

After you read

11 Which of these sentences are not true, and why?

    a Raymond eats the same things on Tuesday and Friday.

    b Charlie wants custody of his brother because he wants the money.

    c Charlie takes Raymond to Las Vegas without telling anybody.

    d Raymond doesn't want to go back to Wallbrook.

12 Why are these things important in the story?

    a the bath   **d** $89,756

    b 21st January 1965   **e** $250,000

    c $93.40   **f** The Beatles

13 At the end, we read: 'Raymond was the winner.' What does this mean, do you think? Do you agree?

Writing

14 You are Charlie. Write a letter to Dr Bruner. Tell him why you think it is better for Raymond to live with you. Tell him about your plans for Raymond, and how you will look after him.

15 Charlie tells Raymond: 'You're like a computer.' Write about the special things that Raymond can do.

16 You are Susanna. Write a letter to your friend about Charlie. Describe your feelings about him. Say how and why Charlie has become a better man since his father died.

17 Write a short story about Charlie's next visit to Raymond in the hospital. He lets Raymond drive their father's car. Where do they go? Do they get into trouble? Does Raymond have a good time or not?

Answers for the activities in this book are available from your local Pearson Education office or contact: Penguin Readers Marketing Department, Pearson Education, Edinburgh Gate, Harlow, Essex, CM20 2JE.